e Swiss

k

ne Martinet
BY URSULA ROOS

icle Books

First published in 1990 by
The Appletree Press Ltd, 7 James Street South,
Belfast BT2 8DL.
Copyright © 1990. The Appletree Press, Ltd.
Illustrations 1990, Ursula Roos used under
Exclusive License to The Appletree Press Ltd.
Printed in Hong Kong. All rights reserved.

First published in the United States in 1991
by Chronicle Books, 275 Fifth Street,
San Francisco, CA 94103

ISBN: 0-8118-0043-1

9 8 7 6 5 4 3 2 1

Introduction

Switzerland is a little country with a population smaller than that of London or New York, yet four completely distinct ethnic groups live in harmony there with four different languages and, of course, with four major regional cuisines. The largest section of the Swiss population speaks German and its cooking shows a marked preference for good substantial fare. The French-speaking Suisse Romande has its own typical regional specialties, while in the Lugano-Locarno region — the Ticino — the people are Italian-speaking and the cuisine reflects the influence of Northern Italy. In the wild mountain fastnesses of Canton Graubunden, where Romansch is spoken, unique dishes are prepared. We shall try to give you a few examples of the wide range of traditional fare to be found and appreciated in this fascinating country.

A note on measures
Spoon measurements are level except where otherwise indicated. Seasonings can of course be adjusted according to taste. Recipes are for four.

Bernese Plaited Loaf

Although originally from the lush farmlands of the Bernese valleys, this golden plaited bread is found all over Switzerland and is delicious for breakfast.

5 tbsp butter	I cup milk
3 flat tsp yeast	2 cups flour
I tsp sugar	pinch of salt
2 beaten egg-yolks	

Melt butter gently in a small pan and remove from heat to cool. Mix yeast with a little milk until liquid. Add the sugar, about half of the egg yolks, the milk and the cooled melted butter and mix well. Sieve the flour and salt into a large bowl. Pour the yeast mixture on the flour. Mix thoroughly. Turn out on a clean, floured board or table and knead until smooth. Leave to rise in a warm place until the dough has doubled in volume (approx 2 hours). Divide into two equal parts and shape into lengths of about I0 inches long. Lightly twist ends together, making a plaited loaf shape. Brush with remaining egg yolk. Bake on a greased baking sheet in a medium hot oven at 375°F for about 30—35 minutes until well risen and golden brown.

Hot Chocolate

2 cups full cream milk
$^1/_2$ cup unsweetened cooking chocolate (preferably Swiss)
I vanilla bean
sugar to taste

Heat milk with vanilla bean and sugar until almost boiling. Melt chocolate in a double saucepan. Remove pod and pour milk onto

melted chocolate, whisking well. Pour all back into milk pan and bring to boil, whisking to form a good froth on top. Serve piping hot.

Four Fruits Jam

This is the thrifty Swiss answer to providing jam for the family when the berry fruits are in season at the beginning of summer. It is perfect for tarts and puddings, and also for spreading on lavishly buttered bread. The taste of the fourth fruit predominates.

equal parts of:	and either:
redcurrants	strawberries
pink rhubarb	raspberries or
gooseberries	blackcurrants
sugar to equal fruit weight	

Clean the fruit carefully, skin the rhubarb and chop into small pieces. Mix all the fruit with the sugar and leave overnight. Next day bring gently to the boil until sugar is dissolved. Boil till set (7–12 minutes) and pour into warmed jam jars. Cover, leave to cool.

Rösti

Swiss Potatoes

Rösti is often called a "potato pancake", but it is really Switzerland's original farmhouse breakfast. A panful of golden Rösti with a cup of hot milky coffee makes a good start to a working day. However, nowadays it is generally eaten at mid-day or in the evening.

Boil some potatoes in their jackets, preferably "waxy", not floury ones. The following day, skin and rub them through a coarse grater. Heat a pat of lard in a heavy frying pan and, when it is hot, put in the grated potato. Press down slightly with a wooden spoon and lower the heat. Fry gently until golden, then turn the "cake" and brown the other side. Add a little more fat if required. Serve piping hot.

Bacon Rösti Add chopped onion and diced bacon.

Zürich Cumin Rösti Add chopped onion and a pinch of cumin.

Cheese Rösti Add slivers of cheese.

Egg Rösti Serve the Rösti with fried eggs on top.

Muesli

The Great Swiss Un-Breakfast

When Dr. Bircher opened his clinic in Zürich in the early 1900s it rapidly became world famous. His treatment was based on radical reform in the eating and drinking habits of his patients. He developed a new dish, which was to replace a main meal regularly. This was a blend of raw fruits and cereals — Dr. Bircher's Muesli. Even today, throughout Switzerland, this meal is called "Birchermuesli" after the great dietician and is not a breakfast dish, but a complete meal, served at mid-day, or in the evening.

Its composition varies according to the season and the fruits available, but the basis is milk, to which are added cereal flakes, generally oats, but also wheat. There is no hard and fast rule.

---

2 cups milk
1 cup cereal flakes (oats, barley, or wheat)
1 cup fruit as available (grated apple or pear, berry fruits, chopped, soaked, dried fruit)

juice of a lemon, or orange
chopped nuts (optional)

Mix, and leave for about an hour to blend the flavors.

Basler Mehlsuppe

Basle Toasted Flour Soup

Basle, the historic Swiss city on the River Rhine, is celebrated for having its own special Carnival in early Spring, dating from the days of the great feasts of the medieval craft guilds. As the pipes and drums start to play at 4 a.m. a heartening bowl of soup is very welcome. The basis of this Basle soup is toasted flour.

---

4 tbsp flour
I cup sliced onions
$^1/_2$ cup robust red wine
I qt beef stock
2 tbsp fresh butter
I thickly cut slice of wholewheat bread per person
$^1/_2$ cup shredded Gruyère cheese
salt and pepper

Heat the flour gently in a heavy saucepan over medium heat until it begins to turn pale golden brown, stirring constantly. Remove from heat. In another pan, lightly fry onions in butter. When transparent, blend them into the flour and then gradually add the beef stock, the wine, and salt and pepper to taste. Cook gently, stirring frequently, for about 30 minutes. Put a slice of bread in each person's plate, with a good sprinkling of cheese on top. Pour soup into each plate and serve at once.

Easter Salad

In Switzerland at Easter, when the winter snows have mostly disappeared, tiny dandelion shoots spring up before the grass turns green again. These are harvested eagerly for spring salad.

---

6 oz loosely-packed young dandelion leaves
I small onion or 2 spring onions
I clove garlic
4 hard-boiled eggs
2 tbsp oil
I tbsp vinegar
I tsp French mustard
salt and pepper

Wash the leaves very carefully in several waters, adding salt to the last water. Drain and pat dry. In a large salad bowl, mix the vinegar, mustard, salt and pepper, and blend in the oil to make a vinaigrette sauce. Add the finely-chopped onion or spring onions and the crushed garlic. Roughly chop the dandelion leaves and put into the bowl, but toss them in the sauce only at the last minute before serving or they will become soggy. Shell the eggs, cut in quarters, and arrange on top of the dandelion leaves. Sometimes fried bacon cubes are added to the salad.

Vaud Leek and Potato Soup

Leeks are said to have originated in Switzerland. They are used in a great many dishes and, in some parts of the country, as an ingredient in sausages. This soup brings out the flavor of the leeks with potatoes in a creamy combination.

---

2 lbs leeks
4 cups water
2 tbsp butter
4 cups milk
1 1/2 lbs potatoes
salt and pepper
1 egg
1/2 cup cream
grated nutmeg
1/2 cup grated cheese (optional)

Wash and clean the leeks carefully. Cut off all the green leaves. Bring the green portion of the leeks to a boil in the water. Remove from heat and strain. Reserve the liquid and discard the leaves. Chop the white part of the leeks and fry lightly in the butter in a heavy pan. Do not allow to brown. Add the water in which the greens were boiled, the milk, and the peeled and quartered potatoes. Season with salt and pepper and simmer for about 20 minutes. Put through blender or food processor until smooth. Return to pan and heat through. Add egg beaten with cream and a little grated nutmeg and serve at once. Serve with grated cheese if desired.

Fondue

Fondue is Switzerland's greatest contribution to party food: it is the ideal meal for making friends. Fondue originated in the French-speaking part of Switzerland, and there are almost as many different recipes as there are Swiss cantons. However, the basic recipes suggested below will be satisfactory.

1–2 garlic cloves	*1 cup grated Gruyère cheese*
1/3 cup dry white wine	*(or 1/2 Gruyère and*
1/2 tsp cornstarch	*1/2 Emmenthal)*
black pepper	*fresh bread cut in cubes*
	(serves 1)

You will need a fondue dish, called a *caquelon*, and a Sterno container to keep the fondue hot during the meal, but the fondue is started on a gas ring or electric plate. First, rub the inside of the *caquelon* with one or two cloves of peeled and crushed garlic and leave them at the bottom of the dish. Pour in the wine, but retain about a tablespoonful and mix it with the cornstarch. Heat the wine gently. When hot, put in the cheese gradually, stirring constantly. Lower the heat and add the cornstarch in wine. Keep stirring until the cheese is melted, the mixture well blended and creamy and beginning to simmer. *It must not boil.* In the meantime, light the Sterno container and settle your guests around it, armed with long forks, piles of cubed bread, and a bottle of the same wine used to make the fondue. When your fondue is creamy rush it to the Sterno container and keep it bubbling gently. Four to six guests share a *caquelon*, each in turn dipping the speared bread cubes into the cheese. If you drop your bread into the dish you must buy a fresh bottle of wine for the company!

Mushroom Fondue A handful of dried mushrooms, preferably morels or boletus, previously soaked, can be roughly chopped and added to the fondue.

Tomato Fondue A half-cupful of peeled and sieved fresh tomatoes with an extra teaspoonful of cornstarch is added to the fondue. Use new potato cubes for dipping, instead of bread.

Herb Fondue A handful of fresh, chopped, mixed herbs can be added to the fondue.

Raclette

Raclette is a dish which comes to us from Switzerland's ancestral way of life. As the snow melts in the spring in the mountain regions, the cattle are able to graze on higher and higher slopes, until they reach the lushest pastures of all at the foot of the mighty peaks and glaciers. The herders go with them, living all summer in high-perched chalets and making rich cheese from the creamy milk. As in earlier days, the villagers go up to the mountain pastures to visit the cowherds and to taste the first cheese of the season. A large fire of dried branches is prepared, a "wheel" of new cheese is cut in half and set before the glowing embers. As the cheese melts, it is scraped onto plates and served with little new potatoes, pickled onions, and gherkins. This is classic Raclette: cheese melted by a wood fire. At home, individual slices of Swiss cheese may be melted gently on fireproof plates under the grill and served in the same manner.

Croûtes au Fromage

Swiss Cheese Slices

This simple dish can be found all over Switzerland and is a popular item on the menu of hundreds of cafes and restaurants, as well as being a standby for the Swiss housewife at supper time.

---

glass of dry white wine (or milk, if cooking for children)
1–2 slices of stale bread per person
mild French mustard
slices of Swiss cheese, preferably Gruyère
(serves 1)

Pour the wine, or milk, into a soup plate. Dip one side of each bread slice rapidly into the liquid, then place them on a well-greased baking sheet, dampened side down. Now lightly spread the top of each slice with the mustard and cover with a cheese slice. Place in a hot oven, or under the grill, until the cheese is melted and the edges of the bread crispy brown.

Ham Cheese Slices Place a slice of country ham on the bread before topping with cheese.

Egg Cheese Slices Add a fried egg to the croutes before serving.

Ham and Egg Cheese Slices Add a fried egg to ham and cheese slices.

Croûtes aux Champignons

Mushrooms on Toast

Switzerland's pastures, mountains, and woodlands abound with a rich variety of mushrooms. Going out to find them early in the morning is a national pastime. However, before filling your basket make quite sure of the species. The popular mushrooms are morels, boletus, field mushrooms, and the lovely golden chantarella. The following recipe is a favorite.

---

4 slices bread
¹/2 cup butter
I cup cleaned mushrooms
(any kinds you prefer or a mixture of several)
I small onion
I tbsp flour
I cup half stock and half dry white wine
heavy cream
chopped parsley

Fry the bread lightly on both sides in half of the butter. Reserve. Chop onion and fry in rest of butter. Slice mushrooms, add to pan, and fry until all liquid is evaporated. Stir in flour. Gradually blend in stock and wine. Season to taste. Add 2 or 3 tablespoons of thick cream. Pour the thickened mushroom sauce onto bread, sprinkle with a little chopped parsley and serve at once.

Lake Perch Fillets

Throughout the summer months, one of the most popular dishes at all the pleasant little lakeside restaurants is perch fillets. Lake perch, still caught in the same type of long net that has been used for centuries, is appreciated for its tiny, tender fillets.

---

¹/₂ lb perch fillets per person

Perch Fillets in White Wine Steep the fish for at least 2 hours in I cup dry white wine. Drain well, dust in seasoned flour. Fry rapidly in a mixture of oil and fresh butter. Sprinkle with lemon juice, melted butter, and chopped chives.

Perch Fillets Meunière Sprinkle the fillets with lemon juice, dust in seasoned flour, and cook as above. Omit chives, add chopped parsley.

Perch Fillets in Batter Prepare a frying batter with 2 tablespoons flour, I egg, salt and pepper, and beer to dilute. Leave fish in this for at least I hour. Cook as above. Serve with herb mayonnaise and lemon wedges.

Omble Chevalier

Poached Trout

Omble Chevalier is a handsome fish of the trout family, with pinkish flesh and a delicate flavor. Fine specimens are caught in the larger Swiss lakes, particularly Lac Leman and the Lake of Neuchâtel. In view of its excellent taste, it is best poached simply in a *court bouillon*.

1 omble chevalier *about 2 lb*	1 carrot
¹/₂ lemon	¹/₂ cup dry white wine
1 onion	5 peppercorns
4–5 sprigs parsley	¹/₂ tsp salt
1 sprig thyme	4 cups water
2 bay leaves	

Slice onion, carrot, and lemon. Combine with water, wine, spices and herbs in a fish kettle or large saucepan. Boil for 30 minutes to make a *court bouillon*. Wash and gut the fish, plunge it into the boiling *court bouillon* and immediately lower the heat. The water will stop boiling but as soon as it starts to bubble again on the lower heat, the fish is ready (about 25 minutes). Check that it is cooked through by piercing near the spine with a fork. Place on a hot dish and serve with lemon slices and melted butter, accompanied by boiled new potatoes.

Grison Beef Stew

This robust beef dish, from the mountainous Grison region, is perfect to keep out winter chills and to satisfy even the hungriest skier after an exhilarating day on the snowy slopes.

---

1 1/2 lb stewing or braising steak, preferably brisket
1 large white cabbage
1 tbsp lard
1/2 cup diced bacon
1/2 cup sliced onions
3 bay leaves
salt and pepper
grated nutmeg
1 cup red wine
1 cup beef stock

Cut out the main stem of the cabbage and discard the thick stems of the outer leaves. Wash well. Boil for 5 minutes in salted water. Drain and reserve. Heat the lard in a heavy ovenproof casserole dish and fry the bacon and onions for 2–3 minutes. Add bay leaves, salt, pepper, and a pinch of nutmeg. Cut the meat into thick slices and place on the bacon and onion mixture. Add wine and stock, bring to a boil and simmer for 1 hour. Now add a layer of cabbage leaves, cover tightly, and simmer very gently for another hour.

Zürich Sliced Veal

This is one of the great dishes of European cooking. It is not difficult but you must work swiftly. In Zürich it is always served with Rösti, but plain boiled rice, or pasta, may be substituted.

1½ lb thinly-sliced bite-sized pieces of veal	1 cup cream
2 tbsp butter	small piece lemon peel
1 onion or 2 shallots	salt and pepper
½ cup dry white wine	parsley

Fry veal quickly in butter until golden. Reserve on hot dish. Fry chopped onions or shallots lightly. Season well. Add wine and simmer until sauce reduces to about half, stirring constantly. Add cream and heat, but do not boil. Add meat and chopped lemon peel. Mix ingredients, heat through and serve at once, garnished with chopped parsley.

Veal and Kidney Slices Substitute ½ lb veal kidney for the same quantity of meat. Fry the kidney separately and add to the dish just before serving.

Veal and Mushroom Slices Fry ½ lb sliced mushrooms in an extra tablespoon of butter with the onion.

Neuchâtel Tripe

This is the national dish of Neuchâtel, that lovely lakeside university city. It is served in all the restaurants of the town on the city's Independence Day, 1st March. It consists of tripe simmered in white wine, served with a piquant vinaigrette sauce.

2 lb tripe cut into 2 inch squares	water
	Sauce:
vinegar	1 tbsp each chopped shallots,
salt	capers, gherkins, parsley,
2 cups dry white wine	chives
2 onions	1 crushed clove garlic
4 cloves	(optional)
2 bay leaves	1 tsp french mustard
6 peppercorns	2 tbsp wine vinegar
1 lemon	6 tbsp mild oil

Boil tripe rapidly in salted water with a dash of vinegar. Discard water. Place tripe in an enamel casserole dish or *caquelon*, add wine, onions, spices, juice of lemon, and water to cover. Simmer gently until tender (2–3 hours). Add salt only when cooked. Mix sauce ingredients in a bowl and prepare the table with a Sterno container, as for fondue, and soup plates. The tripe and broth are kept hot and served at the table over a Sterno container. Each person takes a little, broth, tripe and sauce. The dish is accompanied by boiled potatoes.

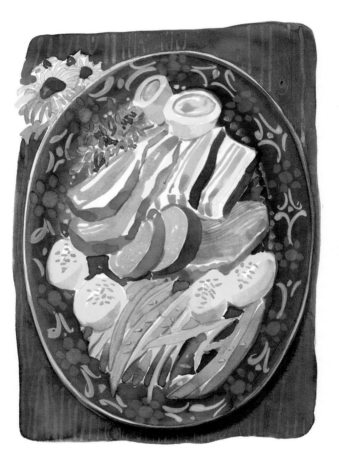

Bernese Dinner

The tale is told that this dish was first prepared for the Bernese troops who defeated the French army at Neuenegg in 1798. It has become a favorite for large parties and family reunions. The ingredients can easily be increased to suit the number of guests. The quantities below are for 8 hearty eaters.

1 lb piece bacon	1 tbsp lard
1 lb smoked pork chops	2 onions
1/2 lb Bernese sausage, if available	1 1/2 pts stock
1 1/2 lb boiling beef	4 lb green French beans, or small
bunches of parsley, thyme,	runner beans
marjoram	4 lb potatoes
4 bay leaves	salt and pepper

Optional extras

smoked beef tongue, marrow bones, salt pork hock
(serves 8)

Soak all salted meats overnight. Simmer beef for at least 2 hours with half of the herbs, and the tongue and hock if used. In a separate pan, heat lard and lightly fry onions. Add the stock, the rest of the herbs, the bacon, and chops and beans. Simmer for 1 hour. Add the Bernese sausage and the marrow bones if used, and simmer for a further 15 minutes. Peel and boil the potatoes. Slice all the meats and serve with the vegetables on a large hot dish.

Fribourg Bénichon Lamb

The great Thanksgiving festival of the Bénichon (blessing) at the end of the summer is held in the Canton of Fribourg. The dish that must be on every table is a savory lamb stew with raisins. It is served with mashed potato and cooking pears, which are stewed whole without peeling.

---

2 lb boned shoulder of lamb, cut in 2 inch chunks
flour for dredging
pepper
I onion stuck with 4 cloves
2 tbsp oil
I leek
I stick celery
$1/2$ cup red wine
2 cups beef stock
bay leaf
sprigs of sage and thyme
2 crushed garlic cloves
$1/2$ cup seedless raisins
salt

Heat the oil in a heavy saucepan or casserole dish, pepper the meat well, dredge with flour, fry rapidly with the onion until it is well browned. Add the chopped leek and celery and fry for about 2 minutes. Pour in the wine, mix well and add the spices, garlic, stock and the raisins. Simmer for 2 hours or until the meat is really tender. Salt to taste at the last minute.

Ticino Rabbit in Red Wine

In the Ticino, this dish is served with Polenta, the golden maize dish which is Northern Italian in origin, but pasta or mashed potato are also suitable. Ideally, the deep red Ticino wine called Merlot should be used in the cooking and to accompany the meal.

I tender young rabbit weighing about 3 lb
$^1/_2$ cup diced bacon
10 small onions
I tbsp flour
I cup red wine
sprigs parsley and thyme
I bay leaf
6 peppercorns
salt and pepper
2 tbsp cooking oil
I cup mushrooms
(serves 6)

Joint the rabbit and dust the pieces in seasoned flour. Heat oil in a heavy ovenproof casserole dish and fry meat until well browned. Remove rabbit pieces and brown the diced bacon and onions. Replace rabbit and pour in the wine. Add spices and enough hot water to cover the meat. Bring to the boil then cover the casserole dish and put in a medium oven at 375°F for 1$^1/_2$ hours. Add the cleaned mushrooms about 20 minutes before serving.

Polenta

While Polenta, which is made from cornmeal, is strictly speaking a North Italian dish, it is served frequently in the Ticino, the Italian-speaking part of Switzerland, where the cooking reflects the North Italian influence.

---

2 cups finely-ground cornmeal
6 cups water
pinch salt
pat butter

Bring water to a boil (in the Ticino 2 cups of water are replaced by 2 cups of milk). Add salt, sprinkle in cornmeal, whisking to avoid lumps. Allow to simmer, stirring frequently, until water is reduced and meal is the consistency of thick porridge. Before serving, beat in butter.

Air-Dried Beef

Air-dried beef originated in Switzerland from cruel necessity. In the early centuries of the Alpine pastoral economy, very few domestic animals could be fed through the long and severe winters. Only breeding stock was kept, the cattle eating what small amounts of hay that had been cut and dried from the mountain pastures during the summer. The rest of the cattle were killed, and the meat was boned, washed, lightly spiced with herbs, and then hung to dry in special drying sheds. These were built on the high passes where the cold wind dried the meat to a solid consistency, while retaining its flavor. The meat was cut in paper-thin slices and eaten raw with onions, gherkins, and thinly-cut rye bread.

Air-dried beef is now a classic starter in Swiss cuisine, particularly in the mountainous parts of the country, such as Canton Graubunden or the Valais. It is the ideal beginning to a Raclette party, and is sometimes ordered while waiting for fondue to be served. With pickles, fingers of cheese, and a little country ham, it makes a tasty light lunch.

The Ambassadors' Mixed Grill

Solothurn is one of Switzerland's loveliest cities, with a superb baroque cathedral, impressive ramparts, and beautiful historic buildings and churches. The town was once the residence of the ambassadors of the kings of France and this dish, *Les Filets des Ambassadeurs,* is said to date from this time. It is, in fact, a lavish mixed grill which is the ideal solution for rather special parties.

---

2 small but fairly thick slices
each of fillet of beef, fillet of pork,
fillet of veal, and one slice of veal kidney
with some fat left on
(serves 1)

Heat the grill and place a large flat serving dish in the oven to warm. Start by grilling the kidneys, then remove and place on the waiting dish. Continue with the pork, the veal, and finally the beef, which should be rare. Have piping hot plates ready and carry everything to the table as soon as the meats are cooked. This dish should be served with Rösti, but new potatoes and a green salad go very well.

Christmas Spice Cookies

This recipe shows the influence of neighboring Germany and Austria where a similar cookie is used to construct pretty iced gingerbread houses. In Switzerland the paste is cut into seasonal shapes: stars, hearts, and so on, are brushed with hot, sieved jam and decorated with colored sugar granules, little silver balls, and chocolate.

1/2 cup fresh butter
1 1/4 cup sugar
3/4 cup golden syrup
1 cup milk
4 cups plain flour
1 tbsp bicarbonate of soda
1 tsp each of ground ginger, powdered cloves, cinnamon

Melt the butter gently and stir in the sugar, syrup and spices. Remove from heat and leave to cool, then stir in the milk. Beat well. Sift the flour and bicarbonate of soda and pour in the liquid, beating vigorously until well blended. Wrap in foil and leave in the refrigerator for twenty-four hours. Roll out thinly, cut into shapes and bake 10 minutes at 330°F. The cookies look most attractive when decorated, and a plateful is always offered to guests throughout the festive season.

Tarts

The delectable tarts to be seen throughout the country are made in round, shallow tart plates on which the fruit, or other filling, is prettily arranged. There are many subtle variations which make all the difference to the appearance and to the taste.

Short-crust pastry:
I cup plain flour
$^1/_2$ cup unsalted butter or vegetable shortening
scant tsp baking powder
pinch salt

Mix flour, salt and baking powder, rub in fat. Add enough cold water to bind to a stiff paste. Roll out to line a 10 inch tart plate.

Apple Tart Peel and core apples and cut into thin slices. Arrange to overlap each other, following the rim of the plate in circles, narrowing to the center. Bake in a hot oven at 400°F for about 30 minutes. Sugar is strewn over the tart immediately after it is taken out of the oven, ensuring crisp pastry. In the vineyard regions, a little white wine, blended with a teaspoon of flour, is poured over the crust before baking and flakes of fresh butter are scattered over the fruit.

Plum or Apricot Tart Proceed as for apple tart but cut the fruit in quarters. Two tablespoons ground almonds or hazelnuts, mixed with 1 tablespoon brown sugar, are spread on the crust before adding fruit.

Rhubarb Tart Use small pink sticks of rhubarb. Wash, skin and cut into small chunks, scatter on pastry. Beat 1 egg into $^1/_2$ cup cream. Bake for 15 minutes, remove from oven, pour egg and cream mixture

on the fruit and bake for a further 15 minutes. This recipe is also used for blueberries and gooseberries.

Cream Tart Mix 2 tablespoons sugar and 1 tablespoon flour and strew over pastry case. Pour in 1 cup cream, cook as before. Cinnamon may be sprinkled over the tart before serving.

Wine Tart Mix 4 tablespoons sugar, 1 teaspoon cinnamon and 1 tablespoon cornstarch. Prick pastry case a few times with a fork to avoid air bubbles, scatter the sugar mixture over crust and cover with small flakes of butter. Pour in 1 cup white wine. Cook as before.

Aargau Carrot Cake

Canton Aargau is composed of Switzerland's most fertile farmlands, celebrated for fruit, vegetables, and the famous carrot cake. Moist, delicious and light, it is completely fat free.

3 large eggs	1 cup ground almonds
³/₄ cup sugar	¹/₄ cup flour
juice and rind of ¹/₂ lemon	1 tsp baking powder
1 cup grated raw carrots	pinch salt

Prepare a cake mold by rubbing the inside well with a drop of cooking oil and then scattering a little flour over it. Preheat oven to 360°F. Separate the eggs and beat the yolks into the sugar thoroughly. Add lemon juice and grated rind, carrots, almonds, flour, baking powder, and salt. Mix well. Beat egg whites until stiff, and fold into the mixture. Turn into the mold and bake for 45 minutes. This cake is often iced with ³/₄ cup icing sugar into which is beaten 1 tablespoon lemon juice. Little marzipan carrots are the traditional decoration.

Spiced Pear Roll

The main ingredient of this cake, made all over Switzerland, is dried pears, which can be obtained in most health food shops. Sometimes dried apples and prunes are added to the pear filling. Small individual rolls can also be made.

---

short crust pastry (see p.48)
I cup dried pears
$1/4$ cup shelled walnuts
I tbsp chopped candied peel
$1/4$ cup sultanas
$1/2$ tsp cinnamon
$1/4$ tsp ground cloves
2 tbsp brown sugar
juice $1/2$ lemon
milk to brush over pastry

The pears must be soaked in water overnight and stewed until soft. Roll out pastry to 10 inches square. Put pears through a food processor and combine with chopped walnuts and other ingredients to make a thick paste. Place filling on half of the pastry square. Leaving an edge of about $3/4$ inch. Fold over pastry, sealing edge carefully with water or milk. Prick top of roll, brush with milk. Transfer carefully to greased baking sheet and bake at 375°F for 35–40 minutes until well browned.

Vin Chaud du Carnaval

Some of the country and mountain districts still celebrate Carnival as in days gone by. On Shrove Tuesday, people in costumes and masks take to the streets and hot wine is prepared to keep out the cold. In our little mountain village in the Valais, Madame Lydie brews up a steaming copper cauldron to the ancient recipe given below.

---

16 cups red wine
6 cups water
4 cups sugar
2 oranges and 1 ½ lemons cut into eighths
a bundle of about 7–8 sticks of cinnamon
(if sticks are not available, a tablespoonful of ground cinnamon
should be tied in muslin and added to the wine).

Heat all ingredients slowly until the mixture is almost boiling, but do not allow to boil. The longer it is left on the heat, the better it is. Top with hot water from time to time to replace loss from evaporation. This old recipe uses no spirits but does have more sugar to give body. If preferred, sugar may be reduced.

Cherries In Kirsch

At the end of a meal, the Swiss hostess will often bring out a pretty glass bowl containing cherries she has bottled in kirsch. They are spooned into small crystal cups, or wide-necked glasses, and eaten by holding the short stalk and nibbling the fruit. Afterwards, one sips the delicious liqueur.

---

cherries
kirsch
sugar
wide-necked, screw-topped jars

The best cherries to use are cooking cherries. Eating cherries become quite tasteless after a few weeks in the liquor, but the tart red cooking cherries retain their flavor. Clean and rinse the fruit. Cut stalks to 1 in long. Allow to dry. Pack closely into the jars and cover with kirsch. Before closing, I always sprinkle a tablespoonful of sugar in each jar. Close tightly. Leave to mature for at least two months.

In the Ticino, dried fruits such as raisins and sultanas, prunes and quartered figs are bottled in a similar manner using grappa, the spirit distilled from the grape pressings after winemaking.

Index